AF367514

After Rain Comes Shine

A poetic collective of life's defining moments

Christel Enriquez

BookLeaf Publishing

India | USA | UK

Copyright © Christel Enriquez
All Rights Reserved.

This book has been self-published with all reasonable efforts taken to make the material error-free by the author. No part of this book shall be used, reproduced in any manner whatsoever without written permission from the author, except in the case of brief quotations embodied in critical articles and reviews.

The Author of this book is solely responsible and liable for its content including but not limited to the views, representations, descriptions, statements, information, opinions, and references ["Content"]. The Content of this book shall not constitute or be construed or deemed to reflect the opinion or expression of the Publisher or Editor. Neither the Publisher nor Editor endorse or approve the Content of this book or guarantee the reliability, accuracy, or completeness of the Content published herein and do not make any representations or warranties of any kind, express or implied, including but not limited to the implied warranties of merchantability, fitness for a particular purpose.

The Publisher and Editor shall not be liable whatsoever...

Made with ❤ on the BookLeaf Publishing Platform
www.bookleafpub.in
www.bookleafpub.com

Dedication

This is for you Mama. .

As bad as I want to breathe, know that I will always love you more.

Preface

Dear Reader,

It would do me no good to say that in writing this collective I came to a final destination that revealed all the answers to some of life's most difficult questions. In fact in most of these poems, you will find depictions of a wandering soul trying to find their way back home, and in doing so I've found that my actions coupled with the people I've met thus far during this journey have continuously broadened my perspective on what it truly is to be alive. That being said, I invite you to come with me as I navigate through the voids and search for light at the end of every storm.

Acknowledgements

I would like to give a special thanks to my family, especially my mom Christel, my uncle Toby, my grandmother Helen, and my brother Dorien. All of you have been my biggest cheerleaders and I could not be more thankful for the love and support you provide. I also want to give a special thanks to my friend Sibel, for being a constant source of light when I needed it most. Last but not least I need to thank my dog Roxy. I don't care how cliche it may be, there is not quite any other unbiased love here on earth than that you receive from your pet.

1. Still Alive

Sometimes an extended period of silence is all you really
need to wake the hell back up
I was gone for a little I guess you can say I was a little
tied up,
yes in a room with white walls
emotions revolved letting me know I was still alive
because otherwise I would feel nothing all

Then thoughts began to sink deep inside my mind,
how did I ever get myself in such a bind?
Yes too many they race all to the same place and then
before I know it I'm looking in the mirror at my own
face,
but I'm not the same person I had wanted to be

This is not the person who always strived to get A's and
B's,
as you were pushed through a system which expected
very little of you, because statistics showed drugs,
alcohol, stealing, death and abuse

Are the reasons your ancestors were slaves and hung on
a noose.

Yes a sick way of reasoning and justification of actions
that taint souls in so many nations,
and then big world problems suddenly become my own
because I now live in the new land of the free right?
So how could anything be wrong?

I take a look around me and hear a familiar song play
through my head "Gotta keep ya head up" Pac said
I would have never thought as I was Jammin in the back
seat all strapped into my little car seat that one day that
very memory would play through my mind
and I would be forced to dig deeper just to find
memories of all the times adversity tried to get the best
of me Only so that I could realize this is nothing but it's
anniversary

Boldness often comes with wisdom and wisdom comes
with time make and loose a few friends work for the
white mans dime People will think they know you

Their thoughts are not yours to take offense, criticism is
inevitable even you have your own sense or feeling
whatever you wanna call it that tells you what's right

and what's wrong or who you can trust vs who's
dishonest

I once laid in a room in a hospital bed with wires, tubes,
and an abundance of prescription meds
not to mention a tumor deep in my head

But this was not the first valley I had to pass through
and as I now stand up right I cant help but ask who up
there was looking out for me because despite all the
darkness thats surrounded me through out my life
goodness which knows no color, raise, religion, sex
or it's orientation has made its way to me without
discrimination

The world would be different
They say it would be a better place
were body, mind, soul, and spirit could bask in grace
and mental health would not be hexed from
conversations leaving its victims trapped in self
sustained concentration camps
I watch as the monitor goes "Beep" and "Bamp" letting
me know my heart is still beating for reasons I could
never understand.

2. Because Humans are born naked

So many times I've hit rock bottom
So many times I've had to get back up
I've seen a few eviction notices
By the time I was 4
I knew what it was like not to even have time to pack up.
I've been hand cuffed and arrested
In my senior year book I was crowned most athletic

I've had my heart broken
I've fallen so in love
I had to learn that sometimes being alone
Is a gift from above

I graduated in the top 3% at RTC
It got me a picture with the secretary of the navy
Even though I daily struggled to March and sing

I stayed to myself and received an accelerated
advancement.
I made friends and lost them over a mental illness I
didn't even know I had
When a tumor caused by stress consumed my cranial
like a new dance.

I ran a mile and a half in under 10 minutes
I was unable to walk after a month of being bed ridden

I've been ostracized and hated
I've been loved and adored
I've spent quality time with my family
I've watched as my parents got a divorce

I changed by baby brothers diapers
I listened as he grew older a spoke with such hate and
violence
I'm now watching him mature and that shit is timeless

I watched my mother push herself to get an education
I've watched from afar as she felt trapped in my old
room of our basement
I listened to her and my father argue over money
because she's always been the one to have to make it

My biological father never wanted me
Another man looked at me and said you will call me dad
He taught me how to play sports while whooping me
when I was bad
But I cannot complain he helped raise me and I'll always
be thankful for that

My youngest sister had a beautiful soul, but kids treat
her like shit because they couldn't understand she has a
speech impediment.

My other sister always worked hard,
harder then most she didn't even know it but about her I
always use to boast
we don't speak now but that does not mean I've crowned
her an enemy
we are on different paths and have different destines

I've raised my hands high in church
but I've been talked about because I married a woman
nothing hurts like the pain you feel when people look at
you with disgust and all your trying to do is be happy,
and work hard to make a living

People say don't put ur business out but they always
stretch an ear to hear what the latest gossip is.

So I've been broken before
I've been down and out
But I'm still here for some reason
so we shall see what tomorrow's all about

So many times I hit rock bottom
So many times I had to search for the light through the
clouds

3. Breaking Chains

The clock moves but the human race is stuck in one
place
no "W" unless we learn to look ourselves in the face
remind you that this ain't really a sprint so please pace
ya self
I'd hate to see you give up tryna save save ya self..

and have patience because this shit is like a spring it
wells deep
yes dwells somewhere in the valley of seeds
and spells that ancestors harvested in hopes that you
would one day bring
into fruition all of the things they could not due to dark
forces and principalities telling them that to think for
themselves meant to rot!

So they lived in fear with shackles and chains they were
striped of their land their blood was spilled from their
veins
torn apart from their families

denied their truth forced into cooperation they are now
me and you..

let that sink in
How does that make you feel?
Can you hear their voices?
Can you feel what they feel?
If you could speak for them would you choose to let the
clock tick in the same old way?
Or you would stand up and move differently
would you peel away all of the constructs that society so
eagerly placed and bestowed upon you?

Or would you take back your brith right?
Are you willing to go the distance are you willing to
fight the good fight?
And I'm not just talking surface level it is a beautiful
thing to have a nice physic
but are you willing to dig deeper?
Are you willing to defeat the things inside of you that
you may not know are there?
Are you you willing to look yourself in the mirror and
I'm talking really stare..

Are you willing to see that maybe there is evil
that maybe you are weak, narssasstic, or even deceitful
to yourself and that maybe the "problem" is not alway

others..

Are you willing to break the curse of your mothers
mother
so that we as a race can go back to the beginning, back
to loving, back to forgiving..

Back to when we listened to the world around us and
had conscious living.
For as above so will be below and waters of life will
freely flow.

4. Window Pane

They say the eyes are the windows to the soul
But have you ever looked at someone
mid conversation and thought to yourself
There's nobody home..
And not in a shallow way...

No im not talking like one of superficial intelligence
But rather depth and understanding
Far beyond this earthly relevance

I'm talking that mind blowing
All knowing
I want and crave to see
Through
All the illusions and fear

All the things that lead to
Emptiness and rework
I'm talking cycles of reincarnation
Where instead of leveling up your coming

Back a mother fuckin carnation

And all though flowers yes are pretty
My friend I desire oceans deep

I crave love and compassion
I absolutely need

Purpose...

My GPS has universal destinations
And I have no time to feel worthless

I've been down that road
And I saw what it got me
but I fought
and I've spent
A whole lot of time reflecting and working
On my autonomy

So you can imagine how important it is to me that my
energy does not get picked off like the petals on a
carnation

no botany..

So yes I wander and wayne and I keep my energy close
to me with tight reins.
Carrying out my conversations with
fellow souls and many
window panes

5. City Walls

White hands on white walls
remember that as the city falls
remember that as they treated us as less
because all we want is to be seen as human beings and
not a threat.
Remember that as they walk around and do as they
please without being stoped while others less fortunate
were instantly shot.
With hands in the air and tears in our eyes
all we wanted was for a world with equality and not to
be stereotypes
Black, brown, and yellow hands built the city
Yet cry's from our inner walls scream iniquity
With words of fury, hate, and scorn
Down come walls that history has worn
Like a bride waiting for an unkept groom
Dividends of freedom eerily loom
In the notion of what is and what was was
May freedom still ring even after the flood

6. Jermie

The thing about angles is they come and they go
One minute they can be seen
The next we don't know
Where to find them
Where should we look
I know I just heard you
Maybe that's why i feel so shook
Because I'm looking and searching
But your nowhere around
I've found traces of your presence
But physically Your nowhere to be found
Maybe I was dreaming
Maybe that's easier to conceive
But turning your memory into pretend will never suffice
so instead I will grieve
I will thank God that You were real and that I witnessed
your being
Your body is no more
But your spirit lives on
Spread your wings and fly dear angle

I know you've gone home

— In Loving Memory Of Jermie Fainning Jr
I will love and remember you always my dear friend.

7. House On Fire

My house was burning down
And I was trapped inside
I began to scream and shout
Help I'm going to die
There were bars on all the windows
So I ran to the door
When I tried to turn the handle
I fell back on the floor
I looked at my hand
My palm was all seared
And then in full blown panic
I burst into tears
Surely I am dreaming
I know this cannot be real
How could I let this happen
I trained and did so many drills
I looked at all my pictures as they came crashing to the
floor
I ran around the house looking for other doors
Everyone I ran to gave the same result

It was getting harder to breathe
I could feel myself choke
All I wanted was to be saved
But no one was coming
I was on my own and I was tired of running
I walked up the stairs only to find one last door
Exhausted and overwhelmed I thought
The end was near for sure
I turned the handle
This time it was not hot
The door flung open
I had finally made it to the top
The difference was I was not running
No this time I chose to walk
It was wretched and lonely
But this time...the door was unlocked

- Inspired by the Buddhist parable of the burning
  house

8. Color Lines

Who am I
Look at me
Sometimes I look in the mirror and even I can't see

My skin it's not light but it's not dark
Who am I
When do I play the part?
I feel the southern breeze skim along the hair on my skin
Yes the heat of the suns rays simmer across my melanin

But those with more
Say mine is no good
And those with little say mine is a product of forbidden
love

So I've fought myself most of my life
I've pretended not to see
I've fought myself..
Who am I?

I have little wealth..
That's what I've told myself
Because the world said so
I've never really had a proper place to go
My skin is not fair
My skin is not succulent black
My skin is caught in between
My existence is trapped

I just want to be
I want to feel
I'm striving to breathe
Do you see me
For who I am?
Will this ever end?
Am I damned
I'm here
I'm breathing
I'm holding on
Please forgive me for I know not what I have or what I
have not

Dear life
Dear race
Dear ethnicity
I am new
And I know all I need

Is love

Tell me on looker

Can you learn to love me?

9. Dissonance

Dear Silence
Im addressing this letter to you because last we met you
told me nothing but the truth
You came to me gentle, tender, and sweet
And you stayed and lingered and guided my minds feet
We walked and you reminded me of all the places I've
been
All the nights that I cried
All the work I put in
And you placed your hand right on top of my heart
And you told me getting back up was always the hardest
part
So I'm staring at you and I'm wondering why
I'm still so afraid to let go and just try
When I already know everything I need is on the inside
Maybe that's why we sit and we stare at each other
because you want me to realize your faith's long lost
brother
A duality that exists to draw us within as we seek the
truths that will save us in the end

So you wipe my eyes and I take your hand and you look
at me
And say

" Now go get back up again ."

10. Locket

Dear lover
I'm sorry for the things I left unsaid
I'm sorry that things turned out so bad
I'm sorry for the pieces of me that I left with you
That now you have to slowly disguard like clothes you
no longer use
Know that although it is over I wish you no harm
I thank you for loving me and I hope whoever loves you
next
Loves you so strong
I hope they love you in ways that I couldn't
I hope they make you smile and laugh because you
deserve it
I hope that one day you think of me as friend
And as we part ways I hope you know I wish you a
happy

11. Solitude

Solitude..
You have been the beholder of solace in the midst of my
own chaos

The gentle reminder that echos an eternity of strength
brought forth through the darkness by my ancestors
before me so that I may relish in times of past and the
days set forth not yet seen air not yet taken in by a
vessel that still for some reason basks in creations being

You are the warm breeze that flows down the nape of my
neck comforting me like sacred sounds heard only by
natures trees
You are the sun that reflects off the waters edge
glistening ever so clear

Your stillness has been sweet yet to my heart holds such
a bitter bitter clutch for I've also had to realize all the
things that I've always run from

You've made me sit with myself
I've cried oceans of tears
I've felt years of pain, and doubt, and fears..
The child inside of me has burrowed even deeper and
solitude you taught me she has so many secretes

Like a flower trying to make it in a storm
solitude..
You have made me try and try so hard
Like an artist that has run out of paint

Solitude you left me like an unfinished landscape
I've left myself and returned
So many times
Rebirth, after rebirth
I'm tired of dying
Tired of lying
So I'm real with myself
This is where I am

A heart full of glass
A mind full of knowledge
A soul longing to be felt...
Dear solitude you are the epitome of cards evenly dealt.

12. Dark Night Of The Soul

Life posses both the beauty and the ugliness of not
knowing
Knowledge is bestowed upon those willing to do the
inner work of uncoding

That is stripping away all of what society tells you to be
and asking yourself the difficult question of who am I
really?..

What do I desire?
What makes me laugh?
What brings me joy that I am able to share with others
you ask?

So I dig deep within..
in search of my soul..
and I find her at times and ask her in frustration why I
don't always know

how to attune to the things I need to grow

And wisdom places her hand upon my heart and says
"dear child love is where you need to start

When you love yourself and find peace within
you will see that all is one and one is all
and all will serve you with the unconditional love that
from your minds eye will never fall.

13. Trying To Escape Dharma

I'm draped in imperfection

I'm smothered in tattoos

I look at my reflection

I see evidence of what someone's else's prayers can do

I'm an old soul

I'm stuck in a foreign world

I am but a trope to modern traces of empathy unfurled

I live in between color lines

I'll never perfectly mold into one universe

I love as if love was blind

I just wish people would listen first

I believe what most deem insane

I don't have all the answers

But I believe genuine living and introspection to be a
guide when darkness advances

14. Trash Day

The trash is building
It's piling up
There's recites and wrappers
Clothes, shoes, and don't forget the stuff that makes you
think yuck
There's I owe you's
Theres exaggerated lies
There's collection notices
And egos that are too big to die
Look at how the trash just keeps piling up to the sky
There's bags full of failures
And that one over there has insults
Don't forget the one that someone else gave you to hold..
Here are the lies and all the insecurities
Over there is physical flaws
Right there is fear and impurity
The one on your door step came from people who you
no longer call
So prioritize your trash the same way it got collected
It's time to take out the trash

Before it gets too hectic

31

15. Scars

You don't just get to come back into my life
and act like nothing happened

This isn't the first time
No this is the second
Wait maybe the third
I've lost track so fast
because
you've shown me
Who you are
As you repeated your actions

With no disregards
Well I am more than just matter
More than just a multitude of atoms

I am emotion
I am spirit and soul
In fact you tried to gain personal satisfaction
By degrading my character

By stomping on my goals

By telling others things about me that amplify
My faults...
By making me think I am worth nothing at all..

Yes the compelling evidence shows my human condition
makes me weak
But my knowledge of life speaks
To my body and tells it stories of other days..
The ones long before and the ones to follow even after
this physical structure decays..

Continuously I change I am trying to grow
I guess you can say I pray?..
Or maybe I'm just reaping what I sowed

I just want to be a better person
Than I was yesterday
So I remember that you too are human
I remember that cuts go away

But scars.. they are reminder not to touch the sharp end
of the blade
So I take my human condition
I take it day by day

And when ever I get discouraged
I look down at the way
scars form patterns of healing in different shapes
And I wear them to remind me life sometimes gets hard

But my soul is still here..
Ironically protected by all these memories and fears
So I'll take your feeble insults
I'll listen to your odious complimentary complaints
Now you can take it how you want it
I am not here to stay..

I just leave you with what you left me

Hopefully striving to be better than you were yesterday.

16. Grace

Sometimes I sit back reflect and just pause
I ask myself how in the world did you make it this far
with all your little inner flaws

then it hits me I been working -
yes working against the laws of gravity

And quiet honestly I think it may be pretty mad at me

Now you may ask

What the heck are you talking about ?
your quiet literally giving human qualities to something
that has no conscious mind or even physical form

Like you have no doubts about what your saying

And that my friends is because I've been praying
And it's lead me to sit with myself
You know silence is one of the greatest forms of wealth..

For it's in the silence that dreams are born
Ideas come into fruition
And fears are torn into pieces
as you look them in the face and let them know

That this is your race
You run this life
You call the shots
You decide which way to go
And which mountains you want to climb to the top of

Just to see there's a lot of
Room left to grow
No matter how far you've come out of
your old ways
Gently moving across this earth with grace
I see you love
And I'm proud of you
Who would have ever thought I doubted you?
Continue forward with all your love
For as below so above

17. Ashley (Little Love)

Dear love,
it's time I gave
a little of you to myself
I'm ready to pull my heart off of the shelf
I'm ready to look into my very own eyes
And dust the corners where darkness
Often consumed the little girl inside
For the me that never really got to be little
Very long
that never got to live out loud
Or sing her hearts song
I'm coming for you
I'm here to save the day
No more hiding little love
Your finally
Safe

18. Painful Surrender

Help
Im falling in love and I've never fallen so fast
It started out slow
Really when I look back it makes me laugh
I met this girl she really caught my eye
So I bought her flowers
I took her on a drive
I bought her a dog
Then we moved in together
I love the way she dresses
She wears all my favorite sweaters
I make her favorite foods
She's never looked better

Her smile is unique
Her laugh is contagious
She's no where near perfect
She comparable to a Classic book
she has many turned pages
But she's all mine and I love her so

From the top of her crown
To the bottom of her toes
Mistakes and all
She's the one
She's got the spirit of a child and her soul it
runs deep so deep I question myself
I look not to others to know my own wealth
I love this girl
I will never let her go
this is the strongest love
Ive ever known
you got to love yourself enough
to be alone

19. Que Será

I looked out my window and saw it was raining
This made feel so sad
I turned to my mother and asked her real stubborn
Why rain existed
She said for plants
She then said for humans and animals too
See water was necessary for us to use
If we wanted to live
We needed it to survive
I looked at my mother
And because I was no older than five said
Why can't we just live off of juice?
She said well baby
Juice is made out of fruits
And fruits just like plants need water to thrive
I said well how come when it rains I can't go outside?
She well baby you never did ask
Then she grabbed an umbrella
And took me by the hands
We went outside

And in the puddles we danced
And she said que será será
Soon the sun will be shinning like a champ

www.ingramcontent.com/pod-product-compliance
Lightning Source LLC
LaVergne TN
LVHW050946200726
843508LV00011B/2460